1970 saw the last of the real two-seater AMX models. Little was changed, but a ram air induction scoop was added to make the hood more aggressive.

In 1971 the AMC AMX ceased to be a model in its own right and was the name for the top model Javelin. Under the curiously-bulbous hood was a choice of two 360 cubic inch V8s with 245 or 290bhp.

More power came with the Go package which slotted a 401 330bhp V8 under the hood and upgraded the wheels, tires and brakes as part of the deal.

1972 would be the last year for the AMX as a muscle car. The Go package was still available but the entry-level engine had been reduced to a 304 cubic inch unit with a paltry 150bhp.

The AMX continued to be sold until 1974, but its days as a muscle car were long finished.

Specification

Years built	1966-1974
Most powerful model	1969 SS
Engine type	V8
Displacement	401 cid
Transmission	four-speed manual
Power	340bhp
Top speed	120mph

The AMX of 1968 was a unique proposition. It was the only two-seater American sportscar of the time

Dodge Coronet

Packing a full race 426 Hemi V8, the Coronet was a mid-size with major muscle

Dodge had used, and then dropped, the Coronet name back in the Fifties, but it returned to grace its new midsize muscle car in 1965.

This car meant business right from the start, being available with the awe-inspiring full race 426 Hemi. This race-bred V8, seriously under-rated at 425bhp, was a little too uncivilised for most folks, though, and the following year saw the arrival of the Street Hemi. Made more manageable by the fitting of a hydraulic lifter cam and a lower compression ratio, it still made the Coronet a fearsomely high performance car.

New for 1967 was the Coronet R/T, marketed as the model equally at home on road or track. It came with heavy-duty suspension and the standard power unit was a new Magnum 440 cid V8, giving 375bhp when fitted with a four-barrel carburator and working through automatic or four-speed manual transmission.

MODEL HISTORY

1965
Coronet instantly stamps its mark on the muscle car scene, with full race 426 Hemi

1966
The Street Hemi is introduced – same engine but a slightly less raw state of tune

1967
Coronet R/T arrives, with standard Magnum 440, and the range is facelifted

1968
Full restyle introduces more rounded lines, but Charger and Super Bee steal Coronet's thunder

1970
Another facelift, but this is the final year of the high performance Coronets

The Coronet range also received a facelift which added such performance pointers as dummy air vents, racing stripes and deep front bucket seats.

A full restyle in 1968 resulted in more flowing, Coke-bottle-inspired lines, but internal competition from other Dodge performance models was looming. The R/T badging was now shared with the more expensive, more alluring Charger and midway through the year the company's new Super Bee undercut the Coronet on price.

The next year saw a new optional engine, the 440 Six Pack, created by fitting three two-barrel carbs to the existing 440 cid V8 and endowing it with 390bhp. The Hemi was still available, along with the original 440, but sales of the Coronet overall were on a definite downward trend.

A restyled front end in 1970 failed to attract further buyers and the R/T and convertible models were discontinued. From 1971 on, the Coronet was only available as a four-door sedan or station wagon and its days as a muscle car were over.

Specification

Years built	1965 to 1970
Most powerful model	1965 426 Hemi
Engine type	V8
Displacement	426 cu in
Transmission	four-speed manual
Power	425bhp
Top speed	130mph

This car meant business right from the start, being available with the awe-inspiring full race 426 Hemi

Dodge Daytona

Dodge's monster racecar for the road was the talk of 1969

Outrageous. That's the only way to describe the Dodge Daytona. Its eye-popping looks and jaw-dropping performance were borne of the company's desire to win races in the hotly-contested NASCAR series.

In 1969, the science of aerodynamics was at the cutting edge of race development, with the slippery shapes of Ford's Torino Talladega and Mercury Cyclone Spoiler gaining supremacy. But Dodge's engineers knew they could do better – and created a wild, 18-foot long supercar in the process.

They took the existing Charger 500 into surgery, adding a wedged nosecone and a massive spoiler at the rear. The Daytona emerged from the wind tunnel with a drag coefficient of just 0.28 (compare that to the modern Dodge Viper's figure of 0.5!).

There would have been even less drag if it weren't for that huge rear wing, which helped to maintain traction on the rear at high speed. And what a high speed! A Daytona racecar hit the headlines with a world closed-course speed record of

MODEL HISTORY

1969
Dodge Charger 500 racecar receives heavy aerodynamic restyle and the Daytona is born

1969
The company has to sell 500 road cars for the racecar to become eligible for NASCAR

1969
The car takes the first four places at Daytona, fulfilling Dodge's racing ambitions

1969
Sales of the street car fail to follow on from the racing success, with only 503 produced

1970
The Daytona doesn't make it into Dodge's road car brochure

201.14mph and another reached 217mph at the Bonneville salt flats.

For the racecar to be eligible for NASCAR, Dodge had to sell 500 Daytonas to the public, so the guy on the street had the chance to buy a hardcore track car that was road legal. The $4,000 price tag was high but not exorbitant, with the standard 440-engined version offering a cheaper option and, with 375bhp, more than enough power for most people. The fearsome 426 Hemi, with its race-bred 425bhp V8, was not for the faint-hearted.

But although the Daytona proved a success on the track, the road car only racked up 503 sales and didn't make it to Dodge's 1970 model roster. The very thing that made it a winner on the track – its aero-dynamic add-ons – proved a turn-off for the public. And so did its habit of overheating at speeds below 55mph – a problem that was solved, to greater sales success, by the next year's Plymouth Superbird.

Specification

Years built	1969
Most powerful model	1969 426 Hemi
Engine type	V8
Displacement	426 cu in
Transmission	four-speed manual
Power	425bhp
Top speed	160mph

A Daytona racecar hit the headlines with a world closed-course speed record of 201.14mph

Dodge
Super Bee

Dodge's answer to the Plymouth Road Runner never quite took off

The late Sixties saw the height of performance mania in the USA, and with the effects of prosperity filtering down to the country's youth, virtually every 20-year-old with a job could afford an automobile.

This was an emerging market that astute car manufacturers were keen to tap into, with Plymouth launching its budget-priced performance car, the Road Runner, in 1968. That spurred Dodge, Plymouth's fellow Chrysler brand, to bring out its own vehicle for giving the kids cheap thrills – the Super Bee.

Released to the public later that same year, the Dodge also shared the same basic chassis, had a virtually identical curb weight, and was offered with the same range of engines as the Plymouth. But the Road Runner undercut the Super Bee's $3,027 base price by $131, putting the Dodge at a disadvantage from day one.

Still, at least the Super Bee looked the part. Bold bumble bee stripes circled the car's tail and it wore a big Super Bee emblem proudly on its flanks. The grille was a sinister matte black and the hood was adorned with aggressive air scoops.

Based on the redesigned Coronet pillared coupe, the Super Bee was offered with only two engines: the standard 335bhp 383 cubic inch V8 or the Chrysler group's prodigiously powerful 426 Hemi.

It may seem strange today, with original Hemi Super Bees hitting prices near to $100,000, but as this engine option added $1,000 to the price, the car's budget-conscious buyers tended to shy away from it.

MODEL HISTORY

1968
Super Bee introduced as a rival to Plymouth's successful Road Runner

1969
Two-door hardtop model joins the original pillared coupe

1970
A restyle and a $64 drop in price fail to stop sales dropping

1970
Wild colors like Plum Crazy and Go-Mango are offered

1971
Super Bee adopts Dodge Charger platform, but the buzz is over

The Bee's low purchase price was achieved by minimising equipment. Automatic transmission was an option from the standard four-speed manual shift, but if you wanted disc brakes, air conditioning or cruise control, the 1969 Dodge Super Bee couldn't deliver.

The same year saw the arrival of the Six Pack engine, as offered in the rest of Dodge's muscle car roster, giving buyers an optional 390bhp powerplant topped off with a wild, air-scooped hood. Made of fiber glass it even had NASCAR-style tie-downs to complete the street racer look.

Although a capable budget muscle car, the Super Bee was overshadowed by the cooler image and greater sales success of its in-house rival, the Road Runner.

Despite 1970's eye-popping color schemes (such as Plum Crazy and Go-Mango) and a switch to the Dodge Charger platform in 1971, the model didn't make it into the 1972 sales season.

Specification

Years built	1968 to 1971
Most powerful model	1968 426 Hemi
Engine type	V8
Displacement	426 cu in
Transmission	Four-speed manual
Power	425bhp
Top speed	125mph

Bumble bee stripes circled the car's tail and it wore a big Super Bee emblem proudly on its flanks

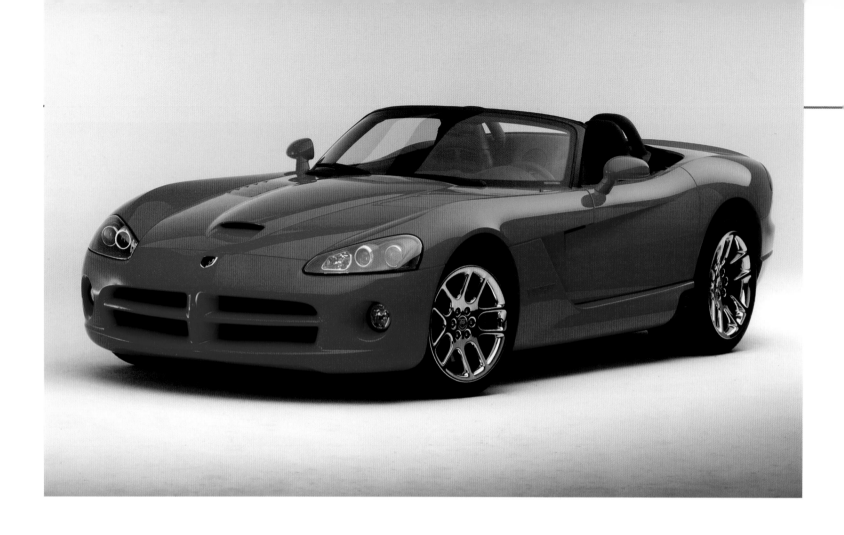

Dodge Viper

The Viper was a concept car made real and it turned round Dodge's fortunes in the 1990s

The Dodge Viper exploded onto the scene at the 1989 Detroit Auto Show and moved the muscle car into a whole new era. Big, brash and brawny, this concept car seemed way too extreme for a company like Chrysler to put into production. But, within three years the Viper was in the showrooms and an American dream was realised.

But it was harsh reality that helped create this dream car, which spearheaded an attempt by Chrysler to re-energize itself. The corporation was struggling in the late Eighties and its Vice President, car nut Bob Lutz, was looking to produce a headline-grabbing sports car to put it back on the map. When Carroll Shelby, the famous Texan ex-racer and creator of the legendary AC Cobra of the Sixties, joined the project, he brought with him a burning desire to reproduce his success in building an iconic American performance car.

Big, brash and brawny, this concept car seemed way too extreme for a company like Chrysler

2003 SRT-10 (left), first gen trio (above), 1989 concept (right)

That was exactly what ended up wowing the crowds at that Detroit Show – the spiritual descendant of the awesome Cobra. A raw, no-frills beast with monstrous power from a huge V10 engine, the Viper's vital statistics were: 488 cubic inches displacement, 400 horsepower and 465 lbft of torque, figures to whet the appetite of any red-blooded sports car fan. The bodywork was pure muscle, a strict two-seater layout fleshed out with beefy haunches and a huge hood to cover that aluminum-block V10 which promised 160mph performance. By the time the first Vipers rolled out of the showrooms, it was 1992, and Dodge's first true sports car for years attacked its task of returning the company to its former glories with venom. As celebrity owners such as Jay Leno snapped them up, Chrysler was suddenly cool again.

MODEL HISTORY

1989

The Viper concept car makes its first public appearance, wowing the Detroit Auto Show

1989

A wave of positive feedback convinces Chrysler bosses to put it into production

1992

First R/T model cars are delivered to buyers. Only 285 are made – all in red

1996

GTS fixed-head coupe version launched with an uprated 450bhp engine

1996

RT/10 upped to 415bhp when side-exit exhausts are replaced by a rear-exit system

Nothing could challenge the Viper's reign as the supreme expression of American automobile performance, and it remained basically unrivalled for nearly a decade. The introduction of the GTS coupe in 1996 provided a hardtop alternative to the R/T model's removable roof and featured an uprated 450bhp engine, but changed little else. The Viper was continuing to prove a popular image-booster but it needed an overhaul to maintain its profile.

When Dodge engineers literally tried to change the car's profile by adding a few inches to the wheelbase, they discovered that they would also need to rework most of the body panels and suspension. So they decided they may as well create an entirely new car: a true convertible with a revised chassis and shell... and an even bigger, more powerful engine!

Dodge realised the passion that the Viper stirred in its owners, so what better way to gauge what the next-generation car should be like than to ask them? The feedback from current owners of the car was resounding: they wanted more power, less weight, bigger brakes and no unnecessary add-ons like cruise control or cupholders. In a true power-to-the-people gesture, Dodge set to its task...

When the new 2003 Viper SRT-10 emerged, it performed pretty much to the brief these owners had given. For starters, it was 100 pounds lighter than the outgoing model. The car still packed a V10 under the hood, but the new engine displaced 505 cubic inches, producing 500 horsepower

and a massive 525 lbft of torque. The previous model's six-speed manual transmission was beefed up to take the extra punishment. A stiffer chassis held everything together, with revised suspension devised to tame some of the Viper's unpredictable behaviour when driven in anger – this new snake would be less willing to bite its driver.

The new suspension also improved ride quality and the brakes received the prescribed attention too, with improved

Nothing could challenge the Viper's reign as the supreme expression of American performance

1997
RT/10 receives the uprated 450bhp engine

1998
GT2 produced in limited number of 100 to celebrate success in GT racing

2002
GTS Final Edition is the final Viper coupe, 360 are made with a red and white striped paintscheme

2003
The all-new 500bhp SRT-10 convertible arrives in showrooms

2005
Dodge announces a new Viper SRT-10 Coupe to be released in 2006

THE ULTIMATE
VIPER

The snake car continues to evolve, and the next expression of the Viper's extreme performance philosophy is the 2006 SRT-10 Coupe. The ultimate Viper, this car is based on the SRT-10 convertible, but with a fixed metal roof featuring 'double bubble' bulges to give more headroom for driver and passenger. That's to allow the wearing of crash helmets – so there's absolutely no doubt about this car's sporting intent! The 2006 Coupe's engine and drivetrain are shared with the convertible, so there's still 505 cubic inches of displacement, 500 horsepower and 525 lb-ft of torque driving through a six-speed manual transmission. But as the coupe is more aerodynamic than the convertible, it will beat the latter's 190mph top speed.

Brembo calipers which Dodge claimed would haul the car to a stop from 60mph in an impressive 100 feet. And the remainder of the SRT-10's performance statisics are equally staggering: 0-60mph in less than four seconds, a top speed of 190mph and 0-100-0mph in less than 13 seconds. The Viper re-established its reputation as the wildest beast in the American auto world with a vengeance.

And the story didn't end there. The SRT-10's colossal rear wheels were the widest available on a stock US production car, at 19x13 inches – and the fronts were no slouches at 18x10. The huge contact area of the tires combined with the car's longer wheelbase made the big snake less unpredictable when really pushed.

The general refinements in the Viper's driving experience were echoed with appointments which made living with a Viper a little less rough and ready. The car was now a true convertible, doing away with the R/T's clumsy removable roof and replacing it with an easily-operated bi-fold

Latest SRT-10 on the road (below and right)

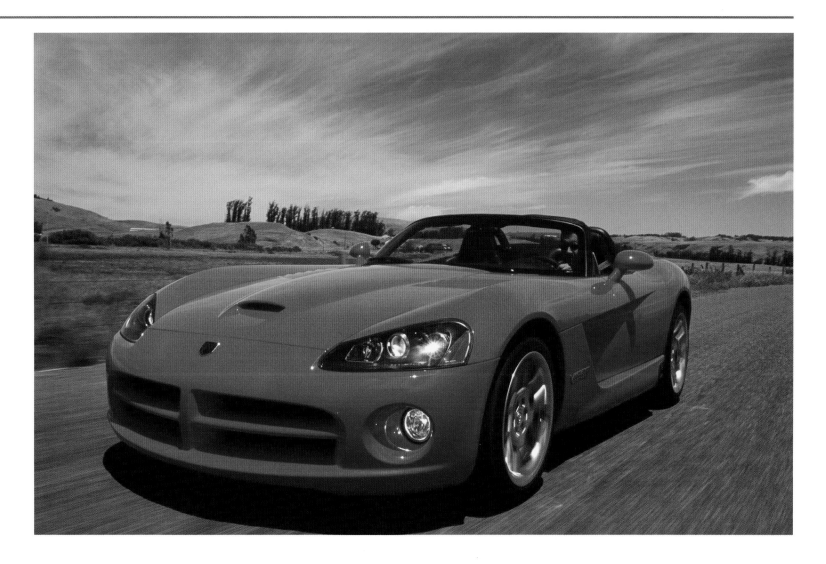

clamshell top which stowed neatly under the trunk lid. The new model also received a serious cabin makeover, banishing the old interior, with its creaky plastics and toy-like gauges, to the garbage can. Now the Viper owner could really enjoy a quality cockpit, rather than have to put up with a low-rent effort. And no, there were no cupholders...

Although still recognizably a Viper, the new model's bodywork was sleeker if a little less muscular than its predecessor. The new conventionally-hinged hood was certainly easier to handle than the old front-hinged job, which really required two people to open without a struggle. But you can't please all the people all the time, and some Viper fans mourned the passing of the 'cartoon muscle car' looks of the original.

Now well into its second decade, the Viper continues to provide the glamour that it first injected into the company back in 1992. Its reliability and longevity has been backed up by repeated success in endurance racing when pitched against the best the world can offer.

The Dodge Viper entered the public consciousness as a symbol of American muscle. With the SRT-10, the legend lives on.

Specification

Years built	1992 to date
Most powerful model	2005 SRT-10
Engine type	V10
Displacement	505 cu in
Transmission	six-speed manual, rear-wheel drive
Power	500bhp
Top speed	190mph

Ford GT

To celebrate its 100th anniversary Ford recreated a racing legend with the glorious GT

The tale of Ford's amazing GT40 has passed into automobile mythology. It's the story of an American company's burning desire to win the world's toughest endurance race against all the odds – a true story of guts and glory. This is a saga of such evocative power that its reprise, four decades after the original events, has led to the rebirth of a legend in the form of the awesome Ford GT.

The story begins back in the early Sixties, when Ford set itself the task of wining the prestigious Le Mans 24 Hour race. By taking the honours in this ultimate test of stamina the corporation hoped to increase sales of its road cars.

In an attempt to fast-track his company to sporting glory, Ford boss Henry Ford II tried to buy Ferrari, the Italian company which had made Le Mans its own with six consecutive victories. Rebuffed by the firm's owner, Enzo Ferrari, Ford

The tale of Ford's
amazing GT40
has passed into
automobile mythology

*Le Mans 1,2,3 of
1966 (above) and
2004's tire fryer
(right)*

determined to produce, from scratch, a sportscar to crush the Italians on the track.

The schedule was insanely tight. Work started in 1963, with the first prototype produced early in '64. After two failed attempts, the 1966 Le Mans 24 Hours ended in a fairy-tale finish for Ford, with GT40s coming first, second and third. In three short years, the company had made Henry Ford II's impossible dream come true – and the GT40 went on to an unbroken string of Le Mans wins from 1966-69.

With its place in sportscar history sealed, it seemed that the GT40's influence would be limited to being one of the most popular shapes on the kit car scene. A detuned roadgoing version of the car had been offered by Ford from 1967, but few were sold and the rarity of these automobiles added to the model's mystique.

MODEL HISTORY

1963

Work starts on Ford's attempt to win the Le Mans 24 Hour race

1964

The first prototype is produced. The car, dubbed the GT40, races at Le Mans unsuccessfully

1966

GT40s make a clean sweep at Le Mans, taking first, second and third positions

1967

A road-legal GT40 is offered to the public with a detuned 306bhp engine. Not many are sold

1969

A GT40 wins the Le Mans 24-hour race for the fourth year running

The rebirth of Ford's legend was heralded by a modern interpretation of the GT40, a concept car shown at the Detroit Auto Show of 2003. The show car proved a massive hit and precipitated the decision to produce a road-legal production model. Symbolic of Ford's greatest achievement, it would provide the perfect centrepiece to the company's 100th birthday celebrations planned for the next year.

Just like its spiritual successor, the new car, dubbed the GT, was set an impossibly tight timescale to achieve its objective. This automobile would need to be ready in a mere 16 months. Considering that it was to be a ground-up re-interpretation of a classic racecar, that was a tall order.

The GT40 formula – a hugely powerful American V8, mid-mounted just behind the driver, clothed in low-slung race-car bodywork – was given a 21st century treatment. But this was to be a road car, so the original's 40-inch roof height (which famously helped to coin its name) would have to be stretched. In fact, the cabin's overall dimensions were enlarged, allowing taller drivers to enjoy the GT experience.

Using the latest computerized design technology, Ford designers and engineers labored to create a modern supercar to evoke the spirit of the Sixties legend. The machine they produced managed to reflect its heritage perfectly, its sleek silouhette echoing the GT40's attitude despite completely different dimensions.

At the heart of the GT is that mid-mounted 330 cubic-inch V8 which sends 550 horsepower and 500lbft to the rear wheels. This high-tech, supercharged example of the engine-builder's art drives through a six-speed manual transmission, putting an indomitable surge of urge at the driver's disposal.

The GT is breathtakingly fast – as a test driver for the American automobile magazine Car and Driver revealed in 2004. He managed a 0-60mph blast in a

Just like its spritual predecessor the new car was set an impossibly tight timetable

2003
Ford's 'GT40 Concept' is unveiled at the Detroit Auto Show to rave reviews

2003
Overwhelmed by reaction to the show car, Ford bosses decide to put the concept into production

2004
Dubbed the GT, the car is the star of Ford's centennial celebrations

2004
The first production cars are delivered to their owners

2005
The GT continues to roll off the production line, a true living legend

stupendous 3.3 seconds and recorded a scorching quarter-mile time of 11.6 seconds at 128mph. Pitted against Ferrari's Challenge Stradale and Porsche's 911 GT3, the Ford wiped the floor with its opponents, the Ferrari only managing four seconds to 60mph and being 0.8secs and 13mph slower through the quarter mile. A Ford GT showed the Italians the way once more!

Despite the monstrous power, you do not need to be a hairy-chested macho man to enjoy this automobile because the GT is actually an easy car to drive. The power-assisted steering, clutch pedal and stick shift are light to operate, with the brake pedal giving access to the astounding decelerative effects of huge Brembo rotors. This is a car that can be as laid-back as a pussy cat, happy to rumble around with a few thousand rpms on the clock, but just as keen to curl its lip and go wild. Fans of great American car chases from TV and the movies will love the tyre-squealing wheel-spin which is available on demand, and all enthusiastic drivers will enjoy the supreme levels of grip and balance.

2004 trio (below), and GT at 205mph (right)

THE ULTIMATE FORD GT

The most successful GT40 ever is the car which won Le Mans in 1968 and '69 – chassis number GT40P/1075. Built in '68, this was one of the Gulf Racing cars finished in the team's famous powder blue and orangeracing colours. With a super-light and incredibly strong aluminium-honeycomb shell, this ultimate development of the race car was capable of a 220mph top speed. When it comes to who's the daddy of all GTs, it's easy – they all are. Ford only offers this modern-day supercar in one version. Guess they think that just owning one of these cars is the ultimate in itself!

With an aluminum spaceframe and body panels, a fiberglass hood and with carbon-fiber used in the underbody aerodynamic system and the seats, modern weight-saving methods are much in evidence. And the modern attitude to comfort is also displayed in this car's interior – with standard air conditioning, adjustable seats and plenty of space, it is a million miles from the GT40's cramped cockpit. The GT's doors are deep cut into the roof, echoing the originals, and another cool feature is that, after hitting the red starter button, you can see the supercharger doing its thing as you sit in the driver's seat.

The end of this story has yet to be written, because nobody knows how long the Ford GT will stay in production. The intention was always that this "Pace car for a whole company" would be produced in limited numbers, with Ford aiming to build around 1,500 a year until demand tailed off. This is one exclusive vehicle, with a selling price of $140,000.

The Ford GT is an incredible feat of engineering built to celebrate a famous sporting achievement.

It is a true living legend.

Specification

Years built	2004 to date
Most powerful model	2004 GT
Engine type	supercharged V8
Displacement	330 cu in
Transmission	six-speed manual, rear-wheel drive
Power	550bhp
Top speed	205mph

Oldsmobile Toronado

A front-drive muscle car? Nobody would have believed it until the Toronado

The Toronado was a truly radical machine. Never mind the amazing styling, the Toronado was the first and only true front-wheel drive muscle car.

The story started in 1966 when Oldsmobile launched the largest front-wheel drive car ever made. It received a fantastic reception from press and the public. Motor Trend magazine named the Toronado their Car of the Year.

With a wheelbase of 119 inches this was one big beast, and at 4,366 pounds it was no lightweight, but Olds gave it serious horsepower to compensate for that. Under that long hood was a 425 cid V8 that turned out 385 hp. And that was plenty.

To avoid too much weight over the front end, the torque converter was mounted behind the engine whilst the gearbox sat under the engine's left bank.

It was an ingenious piece of engineering and laid the groundwork for the American automobile industry's switch from rear to front-wheel drive.

The Toronado's styling was no less revolutionary. It was the work of GM design boss William L Mitchell and he really made this Olds stand out from the crowd. Boldly flared wheelarches, fenders that jutted out aggressively from the front, headlamps hidden away and a fastback tail made this one striking car.

The Toronado was a big hit in its first year of production with more than 40,000 models sold.

A '67 restyle was limited to a new front grille, whilst 1968 saw the Toronado tamed a little. Those stand-out fenders were

MODEL HISTORY

1966
Oldsmobile launches the biggest ever front-wheel drive car

1966
Motor Trend names the Toronado Car of the Year

1968
Restyle tames the Toronado a little

1970
But not for long, GT launched with 400bhp

1971
Second generation emphasizes luxury over muscle

reigned in and Olds' new split grille was added, whilst under the hood a new 455 cubic inch 375bhp V8 was fitted.

In '69 a longer tail was added and so too was an optional, but ugly and quite unpopular vinyl top.

1970 saw a more significant change, with fixed headlamps replacing the concealed ones and the addition of a 400bhp GT version. With a special cam and torque converter the GT could hit zero to sixty in just seven and a half seconds. You could spot a Toronado GT thanks to its twin exhausts, slotted rear bumper and gold paintwork with black stripes.

During the five-year production run more than 120,000 series one Toronados rolled out of the factory. The series two that followed was a shadow of its former self, emphasizing luxury over performance, so it's the original that is the collectors' item. Just ask Jay Leno, he's a proud Toronado owner.

Specification

Years built	1966-1970
Most powerful model	1970 GT
Engine type	V8
Displacement	455 cid
Transmission	three-speed automatic
Power	400bhp
Top speed	135mph

With a special cam and torque converter the GT could hit zero to sixty in just seven and a half seconds

Plymouth Barracuda

It beat the Mustang to market, but it would be some years before the 'Cuda could be considered a true pony car

A true muscle car it ain't – but the 1964 Plymouth Barracuda did beat the Mustang to market by two weeks. Its other claim to fame was its huge wrap-round rear window, said to be the largest single piece of glass ever used on a production car. Initially the Plymouth sales pitch concentrated on the Barracuda's looks and convenience and the most sporty engine on offer was a 273 cubic inch 235bhp V8.

The Formula S Barracuda, introduced in 1965, was supposed to be a performance car. But it wasn't. The most powerful engine on offer was still the 273 cubic inch 235bhp V8 and it wasn't any faster than standard models. There was a facelift in 1966 and the distinctive 'Fish' badges were added.

Then, in 1967, things began to change. The Barracuda had a redesign and it truly joined the ranks of the pony cars. Notchback and convertible body styles were

The 1964 Plymouth
Barracuda beat the
rival Ford Mustang
to market by
two weeks

Plymouth Barracuda 2-Door Sports Hardtop

1970 'Cuda (opposite page),
advert for the '65 (above) and
1970 'Cuda Hemi (right)

added to the original fastback. Plymouth even thought about adding their 280bhp 383 cubic inch engine to the options list. The thought didn't make it to production – the engine was too large to fit the power steering pump under the car's hood.

A 383 cubic inch V8 was squeezed into the 1968 car and coincided with an abbreviation of the name. The Formula S Barracuda became the sportier-sounding 'Cuda with no less than 300bhp on tap. The zero to 60mph dash was accomplished in a reasonably rapid 7.5 seconds. But, despite the power upgrade, the quarter mile was managed in the hardly competitive high 15s.

1969 saw more attempts to make the 'Cuda faster and more competitive with its rival muscle cars. On offer were the 383 V8 with 330bhp and the most powerful engine in the Plymouth stable, the 440 cubic inch, triple carb 390bhp V8 – the largest engine

When the engine shook,
which it did a lot,
so did the Shaker

ever offered in a pony car. With a weight distribution of front/rear 57/43 per cent and no room for power-steering the car was a pig to handle. With drum brakes all-round and no power-steering it was also difficult to stop quickly in a straight line. However the engine helped define the 'Cudas sportier image – zero to 60 took 5.6 seconds and the quarter-mile an impressive 14.01 seconds.

The 'Cuda finally made it in 1970. It was given a new platform, the E-body shared with the new Dodge Challenger. The 'Cuda's wheelbase was two inches shorter, though its overall dimensions were the same. No less than five V8s were on offer,

the most muscular being the 390bhp 440+6 and the mighty 425bhp 426 Hemi. 'Cudas with these engines had tougher performance suspension and the Hemi had a feature that quickly became a muscle car icon – the 'Shaker' hood scoop – so-called because it was fixed to the engine and protruded through a hole in the hood. When the engine shook, which it did a lot, so did the Shaker.

There was also a special 'Cuda for 1970 – the AAR. It was sparked by 'Cudas raced by Dan Gurney's All-America Racers in the Trans-Am races. But unlike the Boss 302 Mustang and the Camaro Z28, the AAR 'Cuda was built as a street rod. An estimated 1,500 AARs were built.

Then in 1971, tougher emission laws came into force. The Hemi was dropped and the remaining engines were de-tuned. Sales dropped almost as quickly as the engine power and the 'Cuda finally died in 1974.

Specification

Years built	1964 to 1974
Most powerful model	1970 Hemi 'Cuda
Engine type	V8
Displacement	426 cu in
Transmission	three-speed automatic
Power	425bhp
Top speed	130mph

MODEL HISTORY

1964
Plymouth Barracuda beats Mustang to market by two weeks

1966
Barracuda 'fish' emblems introduced. Most powerful engine has just 235bhp

1967
Notchback Barracuda joins ranks of pony cars. Performance Formula S version available

1968
383 cubic inch 300 horsepower V8 available in Formula S Barracuda

1969
440 cubic inch, triple carb 390 horsepower V8 is the largest engine ever offered in a pony car

1969

1969 'Cudas sportier
image re-defined – zero
to 60 takes 5.6 seconds
and the quarter-mile
14.01 seconds

1970

'Cuda makes it as a
true pony car as notch-
back introduced

1970

Hemi gets a feature
that quickly becomes a
muscle car icon – the
'Shaker' hood scoop

1970

AAR 'Cuda is the first-
ever production car
with rear tires larger
than front tires

1974

Final 'Cuda rolls off
the production line

Plymouth Prowler

Plymouth's concept car made real may not have had much muscle, but its hot rod styling made it a hit

The Plymouth Prowler looks like a flight of fantasy, a concept car that has just rolled off a show podium. And basically, that's what it is. The Prowler is one of those rare beasts – a concept car that made it into production.

A modern interpretation of the street hot rods of the Fifties, the Prowler made its debut at the Detroit Auto Show of 1993. Jaws dropped, flashbulbs popped and nobody really thought that Plymouth's parent company, the Chrysler corporation, would ever build it. It was just too wild. But they reckoned without Chrysler president Bob Lutz, whose support for the project was pivotal in getting the Prowler signed off and into production.

It would take until 1997, after four consecutive show-stopping performances at Detroit, for this automobile to finally hit the street. But when it did, it remained remarkably true to its original concept.

The Prowler looks like a flight of fancy, a concept car that has just rolled off a show podium

2001 Prowler (opposite page and above with custom trailer) and 1999 model (right)

A two-seater roadster with a manually operated soft top and the sort of radical looks only normally found at hot rod clubs, it was a unique, off-the-peg custom car. For the guy who wanted a street rod but also wanted comfort, reliability and modern automobile attributes, it was a godsend.

The car was the most aluminum-intensive car produced in North America at the time. Most of the bodywork was constructed of this lightweight metal, as was the suspension, helping to reduce weight as much as possible. And it needed to keep itself trim because, unlike its spiritual forebears from the Fifties, it was not powered by a huge V8.

The power unit was the same 3.5-liter (213 cid) V6 found in Chrysler's sedans, producing 214bhp. In the (relatively) lightweight Prowler, its performance was brisk rather than roadburning. But who cared

It remained the same dream machine that inspired so many auto enthusiasts

when you were at the wheel of something this outrageous and getting all the looks?

The Prowler was given a bit more go to accompany the show when a new aluminum V6 started taking care of business in 1998. Power rose to 253bhp, making this a lively but well-mannered roadster. A four-speed Autostick transmission had manual override, allowing the driver to shift up and down the ratios by tapping a stick shift. The ride quality was firm and performance-oriented, although it would be softened down during its years of production.

Originally only available in purple, a whole slew of retro hot-rod colours gradually became available over the car's five-year lifespan, including yellow, orange and deep candy red. Just to underline the fact that this was a car for extroverts, if you didn't already know.

Luggage space was minimal and there wasn't even room to stow a spare tire. The solutions were to offer a matching trailer to give somewhere to stash the valise (an option which 20 per cent of buyers took up) and fat, run-flat tires.

The Prowler ceased production in 2002, and apart from the original engine being upgraded, few major changes were made to the model during its life cycle.

It remained the same roomy, leather-upholstered, electric-windowed, drop-top dream machine that inspired so many auto enthusiasts to take it to their hearts and onto their driesways.

Specification

Years built	1997 to 2002
Most powerful model	1998 onwards
Engine type	V6
Displacement	213 cu in
Transmission	four-speed Autostick
Power	253bhp
Top speed	125mph

MODEL HISTORY

1993
Prowler is first displayed at Detroit and rocks the show

1994
Prototype is taken to hot rod shows to gauge reaction

1996
Official go-ahead for the model is announced at Detroit

1997
First production Prowlers built alongside the Dodge Viper

1998
All-aluminum 3.5-liter (214 cid) V6 introduced, giving 253bhp